Of All the Dirty Words

OF
ALL
THE
DIRTY
WORDS

Richard Shelton

University of Pittsburgh Press

Library of Congress Catalog Card Number 72–77190
ISBN 0–8229–3248–2 (cloth)
ISBN 0–8229–5230–0 (paper)
Copyright © 1972, Richard Shelton
All rights reserved
Henry M. Snyder & Co., Inc., London
Manufactured in the United States of America

Grateful acknowledgment is made to the following publications in which some of these poems first appeared: *Changes, The Falcon, Field, Inscape, Ironwood, Kayak, Lotus, Mill Mountain Review, Pebble, The Seneca Review, Sueños / Dreams,* and *Sumac.*

Some of these poems appeared originally in the chapbooks *The Heroes of Our Time* and *Calendar,* published by Best Cellar Press and Baleen Press respectively.

The poems "Winter" and "Requiem for Sonora" (1971), "Seven Preludes to Silence," "Choose One from Among Them," and "San Juan's Day" (1972), copyrighted © by The New Yorker Magazine, Inc. in the respective years shown.

"The Fourteenth Anniversary" was first published in *Poetry.*

For Brad

CONTENTS

Contents

I

The Dirty Words

here's to the girl
in the high-heeled shoes
the dog in the manger the sparrow
who admitted everything the face
that sank a thousand ships
the village idiot the farmer's
daughter the good men who did not
come to the aid of their country
and Judas Iscariot

whose names are passwords
into the house of scandal
who caught the brass ring of guilt
and could never let go

I drink a toast to your silence

for you the clock on the tower
faces both ways
and every day the roller coaster
says here we go again

as my mistakes line up
in readiness
and I know I will need them
I look back and salute you
with your reasons

let my words be scars on the page
which each of us can translate
into his own pain
and enjoy it
enjoy it

A Toast

I drink to your calumny
who had only one oar
and travelled in circles

you were there when they built
the sea of regret
and every night you return
to find it waiting

The clock drips
like a familiar faucet.
In the dream you are always
falling, falling,
but never into anything.

Tomorrow waits
on the other shore which
smells faintly of sulphur.

Take a card, any card.
It will be what you
have always dreamed of.

his gloves were meant
for better hands
his hands for better gloves

the story of his life
gets smaller and disappears

when spring arrives
who will support the cause of snow
hanging like a sound from a trumpet
frozen in the distance

and how can water live that way
without asking permission of anybody
a quiet voice with a short memory

who can it love
attracting light
and the moss beneath it
as soft as a snail's foot

the eyes of stones
even if they cannot see will listen
with all the senses of their colors

and ghosts of sycamores
will wait for darkness
when they can embrace each other
like smoke

but winter has looked
into so many houses

he knows that when you are poor
nothing is ever enough
and when you are rich it is the same

SUICIDE

He finds himself eating among the mouthless
and singing for those who have no ears.
He hears the soft death rattle
of frightened leaves. The place where
summer should be is gone.

He says, "Who will comb my hair?"
Only the water answers. All day the waves
beckoned to him but he was afraid.

Now it is as if he had an appointment.
He thinks how perfectly water
will adjust to the shape of his body.
There will be no incisions, no scars.

His divided heart, caught in a cage of ribs,
hears music. The water is full of bells.
He listens for music
as an addict listens for the rush
in his veins. Naked, he steps into refraction.
His feet are whiter than sand.

He stands like an island off the coast
of despair and his lover kneels before him.
She fondles him, circles his waist
with her arms. Slowly her lips rise to his.
He goes down to her singing.

you still carry
your guilt around for company
I will not deprive you of it
but I have an empty space
where my hate lived
while I nursed it
as if it were a child

brother my only
brother it was too late for us
before we were born

it was too late
before you learned to be brutal
and I learned to be weak

your childhood
was a hallway of doors
each closing just as you
got to it
but I was younger
and all the doors were closed
before I could walk

how could I have expected you
to save me when you could
not save yourself

brother my only
brother if not from you
from whom did I learn
so much despair

I went in search
of a father and found you
with a whip in your hand
but what were you searching for
in such dark places
where I was searching for love

each day the terror wagon
passes while elevators
hesitate between floors
and frightened windows
cover their eyes

the bell rings *bring out*
your dead bring out your dead
the bell keeps ringing

we are sad quiet men
in a difficult century

we run our treacherous
fingers through their hair
one last time
and trade our children
for the most expensive
versions of old lies

a bruised moon comes up
pointing one pale finger across water
where the lake is chained to its bed

silence
crawls out of its nest among the explosives
the emptiest drum speaks
loudest *the revolution the revolution*

having knelt all day
at stations of the animals
members of the society for the prevention
rise with guns in their hands
while mothers and children hide in the cleavage
between scarred breasts of hills

in the eyes of death
a dreaming star waiting to be fulfilled

the wounded
crawl through fields of bleeding turnips
trying to remember
the famous last words of the snow
and in the distance tiny puppets
lean from their windows
shouting *fire*

refugees notice that their feet
have walked through their shoes and disappeared
they find death a convenient way to travel
and move on without bothering
to take their bodies

Revolution

new masters find old voices
with which to address the people their faces
will soon appear on the money

but only whispers circulate
in the houses of the newly undiscovered
they are waiting
come the revolution

a little earth
left in the tabernacle of earth
a little water in the sanctuary of water
where the wind is an anchorite
with uncombed hair

these cannot protect themselves
and have lost even the ability to hate us
their murderers

will they return
after we have finished building
our monument to a dead clock

The man who repairs everything
will be here tomorrow. We will
tell him about the oven.
We will tell him about the purple
veins in the water, the milky
light, the bruised hibiscus.

He will take tools out of his truck
and begin to repair everything.
When he is finished we will say,
"Wait! There is more." We will
ask him to repair our lives,
to fill up the intervals within them.

He will explain to us
how some faces are always luminous
in darkness, some flowers open
only to the moon. Then he will
get into his truck and drive away,
and we will know how easy it is
to live. We will be happy.

in some things there is a pride
which cannot be destroyed by design or accident

the pride of a house to which no road leads
the pride of hair which continues growing after death
the pride of trees whose leaves
are a mystery for dawn to explain
the pride of water with its temporary scars

the pride of a young man
hired to make love to women not easily satisfied
the pride of the princess who hanged herself
not because she was captured in battle
and sold as a slave at auction
but because the bids were so low

the pride of steps ascending to a beautiful door
whether the door is open or closed
the pride of tiles in their obedience to a pattern

the pride of a dead poet
whose eyes look up from beneath his words
as if from the bottom of a pool

the pride of a canyon so narrow
the river must turn on its side to pass through
the pride of the rattlesnake who warns his attackers
the pride of the coyote who moves away
to a safe distance but no farther

the pride of Narcissus
a white face with petulant lips
seen always in profile under the curls of a god

I who threw a pair of dice into the sea
and found them on a beach years later
with the winning combination uppermost
can say this quietly
if I can say it at all

as we drive past calcium water
you notice on its shore the dead foundations
of a city built with sand
cement and tears

what kind of place is that you ask
not knowing I could take you there
and call each ghost by name

if I fail to answer your question
it is not because I have come a long way
I have come all the way
and each day I have it to do over again

giving one cry
at the limits of the human
and hearing it repeated casually by a bird

I accepted words from those who spoke
and silence from those who were silent
I voted for no one but somebody
voted for me
and I am here as if I had made the choice
as if I had been elected

facing success
the dirtiest of all the dirty words
the only adversary worse than failure

and how foolish to ask myself was it worth it
when I can no longer remember what I
wanted or why I wanted it

parts of me were left along the way
a foot here an arm there
I cut my losses

and perhaps someday I will be able
to tell you the story of my other life
pretending it is someone else's
some haunted friend I knew years ago

you will cry a little and say
how fortunate we are

goodby was never an easy number
except to the distant
except to those already gone
except to those in love with some other place
and eager to be there

my plans are mine
I will not let dawn interfere

what did I want to say to you in the darkness
that cannot be said in the light

imagine the famous coloratura
with her legs in the air
in the ridiculous posture of sex
her high notes scattered like cards
and the sweaty hands of the dealer approaching

imagine your daughter
halfway between innocence and the tall grass
your son in the arms of a crone
with bloody fingernails
imagine yourself
padded and rouged in a coffin

sooner or later somebody knocks on the door
looking like anyone else
and bringing disaster

II

The Other World

I can tell you this much
without incriminating anyone:
There is another world.
In that world the dust
pleads for attention
and the bones of one skeleton
are always tangled
among the bones of another.

The eyes of those who live there
are as blind and fragile
as eggshells. Pain is visible
in the twisted fingers of their hair.
Nothing is repairable.

There is a lighthouse in the desert
with black gulls wheeling around it
screaming for rain.
Tall minarets of fire
rise from withered sand.
We build bridges to attract
a river but none comes.

By day there are academies of silence.
At night we hear the hungry
bleating of carnivorous lambs.

If I told you the truth
about everyone who lives there
you would believe me. You would
cry a long time
but you would believe me.
You would never be the same again.

Wisdom is the knowledge of alternatives
and I have none. Which fine print
did I neglect to read?

After so many years
of walking in the wrong direction
my swollen feet remind me of the distance.
I arrive at the reunion of empty shoes.

The latent are here: sadness
madness apocrypha
the disappearing train
the blind voyeur
the dry wash
the dead horse
and those who have tasted
damp curls under the arms of a god.

They are at the door this moment
calling with a small voice
but so terrible.

as long as the question was unspeakable
the answer was silence and I
lived with the silence as if among friends

it took years of practice
to learn to hold fire in my hands

but when the scars healed a little
I heard my voice approaching
from the distance and I listened

now I have forgotten how many hours
are supposed to elapse between give and take
I have forgotten the reasons for waiting

aged beyond recognition the future
hobbles away and I call it the past

I drag from beneath each stone
some dirty old memory screaming
and shielding its eyes from the light

this is work suitable to my weaknesses
to classify specimens
in the dark categories of love

where the pig goes to the market
the pitcher to the well and the truth
of the matter is they will never return

1

something in the sea hates us
knives of light rise from water
each wave lopes toward us
frothing at the mouth

when the shadow
of the great fish of darkness
swims slowly over us
we will turn our eyes for comfort
to the moon

2

a sailboat moves before us
translucent blue shell
all our descriptions of this silence
will be inadequate

time stands on one leg
at the edge of the bay
watching us as if we were real

bone shell
false light dying planet
the beautiful is already upon us
how can we tell it to go away

3

we will remove our folded embryos
from dresser drawers
and travel inland
to practice exercises in self-belief

when we are gone the sea will remain
saying nothing nothing
to so many others

THE DOUBLE

few of us have a choice
and fewer still refuse to make it
but he could not live in half a world

he moves through many lives
like light stepping across water
leaving no proof he was there

he inhabits the houses of others
as if they were built for him
and when he leaves them
he never returns

the side effects of his debaucheries
support him as a saint
the hourglass he carries
holds equal parts of suicide and wine

his existence is doubled
he takes twelve hours a day of dying
and in return he gets
twelve hours a day of life

LETTER TO A LOST FRIEND

War, trade, religious debts to
discharge, these are mostly the
reasons for men's distant journeyings:
but you take pleasure in distant
journeys without reason.
St.-John Perse

we do not realize what we want
until we learn
what we are willing to give up for it
and you did God knows you did

when swimming was no longer possible
you learned to sink you learned
to live at the bottom of the sea

now tell me of the chambers where you sleep
tell me it does not matter
lie if you must

is your bed luminous is it festooned
with seaweed do all your narrow windows
open onto water
is the tide kind to you

forgive me if I do not understand

last night a stranger asked me *what
gives you most pleasure* and before I thought
I answered her *revenge*

So here I am the fair-haired boy
on his way to the river, a short journey
to a foregone conclusion. With these faded
tattoos, miscellaneous scars and stigmata,
a little flesh left to mortify, I am
asking the same question of everyone:
What did I use you for?
And from each I get a different answer.

Whatever I dropped to mark a trail
the birds have eaten, they are welcome to it.
I will not be returning this way
where the trees above me are strangers, a little
evening light brushed on their leaves.

And just as the wind loses all its ambition
I lie down with the pilgrims who sleep
in the park. They know how to face the hat rack
bareheaded, how to live off the land.
Believers supply them with gods.
Gardeners who irrigate leave pools of water
as gifts for their feet.

Together we cultivate silence and the dark
innocence of grass. We practice sleep,
the ability to stay under water.
We are mosaic figures on the floor of the sea.

We have heard the song of the descending
belt, we have heard scholars
pursuing savage bibliographies
through thickets of privet and oleander.
Now we hear young leaves who suddenly begin
to talk to one another as if many delicate women
dressed in silk had just entered a room.

The moon arrives like a blond caryatid
telling apocryphal stories. We listen
and we believe. She tells us that those who walk
all day on razors lie down at night
on beds of wet salt, that our ability is silence
and going away. She tells us that random
numbers wander in search of order.
She tells us of deep trees, reaching down
into the earth's blood, of the lichen's tenacity.

By the time dawn has made its final decision
those who are wise among us have lost their
memories, those who are greedy have sold them,
those who are cruel have given them away.
I see that each of us carries a stone
inscribed with his destination. Mine says
to carry a stone to the river. It is
so easy now and I start out like a moth
on his final journey into the thorns of light.

are so thin they can stand
in the rain without getting wet

when they walk on the beach
they see each wave
leaping over the bones of its father
and as the bones melt they see
beneath them the teeth
still smiling

the heroes of our time
know the intimate gestures of trees

when the wind approaches them
rings grow on their fingers
carnelian amethyst topaz

when they speak and when they listen
it is always with their hands

when they fold their arms
they express a great silence
and we who complained
of the promiscuity of lightning
begin to experiment with flints

the heroes of our time
are clarity surrounded with darkness
need in the absence of prayer

light runs through their veins
and returns with the answers
to their questions

when they die
their names are buried
under hidden monuments but their
bodies are scattered on battlefields
and soon wheat grows again
in the ruined fields

the wheat bows to the wheat
and is harvested and a few grains
are left on the ground
to be gathered
by the heroes of our time

This is my flesh, neither
unloved nor unpaid for. These
are my bones underneath
with feelings of their own.

Sometimes I do not listen
to what is being said to me.
When I touch you I wear
masks on my hands.
Forgive these mild excesses.

Once I believed as other men
but I got over it. Now
I accept the darkness
which belongs to me. What else
of value can I offer you?

When I came to the temporary
river I was going nowhere
in particular. It was
deep enough to drown in
but I swam across it.

Now it has forgotten its source
and lost its destination.
I return to find it gone.

Is there a chant strong enough
to exorcise what haunts me?
I arrange and rearrange words,
hoping to find the incantation.

Something about how trees
accept light. Something about
the promiscuous intercourse
of water, the celibacy of sand.

I search for the barest place
to live and find the ruins
of ancient houses facing east.

this is where the tar and the feathers
and the autographs
settled for the night
I who was unforgettable in my time
have been forgotten

each hair on my arm
still lives in its enraptured kingdom
these are the gears of my hips
and my legs secretly married to one another

my youth was a preparation
for a priesthood
to which I was never ordained
I was waiting for a train and looking
forward to the journey
when suddenly the depot disappeared
taking all my luggage with it

sometimes I think
the smoke must love the chimney
but it goes it always goes
leaving an old candle
under the branches of dead trees

each day the light takes advantage
as if it were innocent
as if it did not know what it was exposing
and at night I watch the moon ripen
hoping it can stop in time

is it because I was more thoroughly looked at
or because of what I have seen
that I have spent years
trying to learn the art of silence
and failing

I left the scene of the battle
and retired to more violent diversions
where the last card is always the dirtiest
but those who have nothing to be ashamed of
have nothing
how can the poor in spirit
afford such suffering

CODA

be private
let no one but strangers touch you

go out in madness
and observe the lidless eye of the moon

return in madness
wear madness under your skin

compress failure into a stone
compress the stone into a jewel

crush the jewel into dust
and eat the dust

learn to feed and water silence
be merciful to trees which shelter you

kneel at the feet of mountains
guard the desert while it sleeps

III

Home to the Ruins

well old place I am back
and I notice your trees have been growing
while I was gone
providing more shade
to keep up with the needs
of those recently buried

this is where my story began
although I was not
consulted so I ran away

but I have returned
to fumble among the bedclothes
of the dying and I will do it again
will I do it again

carrying three finger bones
of an anchorite lost in the desert
and my lottery ticket for a second chance
at an earlier disaster

city of the eternal triangle
Adam and Eve and Pinch Me
I was always Pinch Me

city of trees
we have both changed
some would say for the better
but how strange to find you soliciting
for my cheap triumphs when you were always
a purveyor of regret

someone has torn down your mirages
to build new mistakes but I remember
these charcoal gardens
I helped set the fire I remember
your citizens
crookeder than threepenny knives
your children hanging from nails in the wall
I was a child among them

I have been here all day
waiting for the son of no one
for the son of anyone for the son
even of despair
waiting for myself
like a stone for the chisel
when the truth is
my statue was finished years ago
and you were the sculptor

under the stained-glass window of evening
before night arrives
now it is time
and I can no longer remember when it wasn't
to tell myself I am some kind of man
the kind you created

clay-foot city my place of birth
release me today of all days
between the full bottle and the empty glass
while arthritic light
hobbles down the road on its crutches
slowly down the road
and over a blue-blooded hill
going home to the ruins

my father died
having given the matter much thought and decided
having first released me from the commandment
having become the child he knew I needed and I
                              carried him in my arms
leaving me his childhood because mine had been
                              taken from me by others
showing me the proper way to die because I did
                              not know how

my father died
surrounded by those who loved him and they were few
surrounded by those he loved and they were fewer
leaving no division among us for there was nothing
                              to divide
and the earth which we had already divided unequally
        accepted him who had no part in that division

my father died
and the neighbors went on fighting but the rain
        which was to come would calm them
and the tools he had handled went on living
        in the hands of those less competent
and no sympathy was called for so none came

my father died
leaving the question of darkness to the darkness
                and the question of light to the light
and the pain which had lived in his house had
nowhere to go so it died with him and was buried
barefoot because he had not worn shoes in a long time

my father died
having arrived too late having arrived too early
having been absent most of his life and otherwise
                              at the wrong place

my father died
the night the saints rise from their graves and he
            passed them moving in the opposite direction
holding one hand out to the window and saying words
I could not translate having already told me all I
would need to know but would not remember until later

my father died
before the rain came but he knew it was coming
and the rain which had been waiting fell on us
                        to make it easier
and dust settled on the eyes of the water
            but the water did not close its eyes
and hoops fell from the barrels and rust arrived
            to take possession of its country
and all his lives died and some are easier
                        to forget than others

my father died
in bed and sober who would have preferred to die
            drunk and on his feet in a bar
and those who had known him as someone else
remembered him in places I had never been
and took nothing from me and would have given me
            all they remembered if they could

my father died
having received what he had waited for and whatever
it was I gave it to him and we both knew he would
take it with him and it would never be a burden to
                        anyone else again

my father died
poor and the mourners came and went away quickly
but all night the stones were opulent with rain

Lady of mint beds and violent
gladioli, who fought off
the birds for every strawberry
and the hunters for every bird,
a splintered hip grows in your garden

but do not pity it. Your three
husbands will tend it as you
kept their coffins supplied
with clean sheets. Pity

the mice who never built nests
of your fine white hair and the bats
who never got into your belfry.
All these years, Lady,
they have been homeless.

THE CONFERENCE OF FRATRICIDES

for My Brother

I beat my memories with whips
to keep them alive, expecting
to find you waiting for me someday,
after dawn in an old house
with its dead lights still burning.

I thought we would sit
at either end of a long table
with a gun between us.
We would stare at one another,
comparing our identical birthmarks,
each of us wondering:
Which part of me are you?

You would tell me the myth
of paradise. I would tell you
I had been to the land of voluptuaries
and found it ruled by pain.

I thought such rituals
were necessary before death,
but instead I find you sleeping,
fat and comfortable, on the velvet
of old dollar bills.

There were so many times
I tried to kill you, but you wore
your sleeping innocence like teeth.
You never knew.

is always of course a dream
and determined by little things
years ago

it could have happened
in a porch swing or the back
seat of a car but it didn't

I kept an appointment
among wild syringa beneath the pines
it was late evening almost dark
with the moon in its cradle

I remember the smell of leaves
coated with dust but who was it
who was it
can I admit I do not know

tonight
mad harmonicas play in the streets
resurrecting the dead

the moon twitches
like the flank of a stallion
toxic with power

we have been following footprints
on the surface of bent water

we come home late
we come home quietly
carrying our shoes through burnt silence

we come home to despair who has
waited up for us

there goes the story of my life
old failure
with a new mask on
looking as innocent
as the scene of the accident
before it occurs

the one who pawned his best
opportunity
sneaking back
with a ticket in his hand
thinks nobody will recognize him
thinks he will get away with it
while the wind
rushes after him doing
the same old schottische
putting its little foot right there

my life
who made few promises
and kept none
is moving from left to right
past doorways which expect him
at any minute

he used to live on this street
and now he is
returning
while his voice spreads before him
as contagious as sunlight on water

he knows
everything about this street
except its destination
these houses with the elegance
of the grotesque
flooded basements embedded with faces
the glass coffins the pillars
revolving slowly the rusty
light in the hallways
the screams
arriving like guests but who
invited them

coming back to his elders
the drunk and the sober
to those who told him
what it would be like and it wasn't
to those who told him
lies of all colors
dreams fantasies fictions

he returns
in search of a new name which will
look better in the photographs
he returns like recurring madness
to the bosom of the bosom
of the family

as the moon strikes
the hour of the empty bottle he
returns like a siren
stopping at a familiar address
and he gets out
with his nightstick in his hand
to go in and break up another fight

WHY I NEVER WENT INTO POLITICS

for Brad

my son
I promised you a world and see
it is all gone it is beyond
repairing we must learn
to live without it

each day a parade of soldiers
goes past followed by dogs
whose clinking tags proclaim
they have owners
and they are not mad

we are told not to look up or down
the sky is not public the earth
is not ours
we are told to look
straight ahead and march forward
and kill
that is the way it is done
in this land

my son
I love you and having told you
all I remember all that is left
of an old story
I tell you that those
who use the language of poets
are poets and those
who use the language of thieves
are thieves

in the distance
some band is playing

a march
which started out as a waltz
and got carried away

and we are marching

the next victim steps up to the wall
his face as familiar as a bruise

the cards are all dealt and me with no hands
the ink blot which tells my story never appears

outside I am trying to remember
inside I am trying to forget

in the kingdom of hidden tattoos
I could not wait to sell my memories
I gave them away
but I kept my doubts for future security

I am not worthy of speaking a holy name
to protect me
but if I knew one I would say it anyway

my shadow leans against a table
a little man with his extra hands
in his extra pockets
like a guest without responsibilities
complaining of his treatment

all day we climb a ramp
single file
each with his burden
like Egyptians building a tomb

seen from a distance
our postures are stylized
and beautiful

but having begun
such a promising journey
we discover we are going
to market to market
to find it has closed

we sit through the night
in a bus station
each with his stolen eyes open
and a dead bird in his lap
while a voice calls out
the destinations the names
of minor battles in famous wars

we are tired
surely if there is one thing
we want more than anything else
and we give it up
we will be almost happy
the rest of our lives

Under a mandala of revolving
stars he moves west toward the last
beaches, still looking for something
to wrap in his piece of flannel:
a violin, a machine gun, a child . . .

So young to have surpassed his masters,
blindness his master, hatred
his master, pain. They smelled
success on him early, like tar.
He invented the hallway of mirrors
and put himself in every frame.

When he arrives they greet him
with cameras and contagion. They
are making a movie of death. He lies
on the beach under an old umbrella.
Among sand dollars embossed
with ancient flowers he finds
bits of bright glass and lost mustaches.

The rhetoricians announce beauty
to the sound of drums. The director
shouts over a bad connection.
The final pose. Flex! A little
muscle music for the late Mr. America.

For a long time voices
had been gathering around the ultimatum.
They were shaped like lips.
They got ready.

The war ended but we
could not go home. None of the roads
had names. There was a final
whirring of clocks. The lights
went bright for a moment, then died.

Night came too early
to be of any use. It stood
around disguised as possibility,
like an unfinished gesture. We tried
to shield our eyes from the darkness.

It was not a question
of what would happen to us. Nothing
would ever happen to us again.

But the last season arrived
smiling and with such splendid teeth.
It reminded us of the lives
we had spent between sewers
and chandeliers, changing our clothes.
The mirrors had gone out
and we saw ourselves reflected
in one another's faces.

Some fool shot the president,
thinking it would help. By then
the rest of us knew that all
our windows opened on the sea.

We are rich sons of rich
fathers. We have inherited the earth.
We stand in a row awaiting
our posthumous honors. Between
intervals of silence we hear
someone bleeding. Is it
only the death of language
that makes us cry?

THE SOLDIERS RETURNING

it was almost easy to say goodby
we said it we kept saying it *goodby*
goodby no one was listening

we travelled
pretending we were pursued by something good
in spite of empty horizons

we stood on the parapets of distant hunger
and slept in strange beds
in the red-light districts of the impotent

sometimes we knew
what we were doing and did it
sometimes we were not sure

now we return as the white hand
returns to its glove
and how to convince the darkness we are here
when it has so many others to care for

we return bearing the secret
that there is no secret
no collusion no plot
wars occur because men want them
and peace occurs when they are tired

we who were hired to kill
but not by anyone we could name
not by anyone we could talk to about it
return to the terrible menace of love
and to our children

1

All day a wounded mountain followed me,
gentle and crumpled like a fern.
It was too shy to speak of its great need
and what could I have done to help it?

2

The desert has forgotten what it is waiting for.
Even sand will not survive without a purpose.
Can dust learn to swim? Will flowers
be able to repeat themselves in stone?

3

We have removed the earth's flesh and torn out
its bleeding veins. Sunlight reflects
from our knives. It blisters the surface
of the lake where nebulae of fish will never
return. A few gulls carry their white grief
on delicate hollow bones from water to water.

4

We have forgotten that once there were black
swans with brilliant red beaks and curly
tail feathers. Soon the last birds of desperate
passage will ricochet through our oily rooms.

5

The stars confirm nothing, deny nothing. Heads
of animals grow on our walls. Their hopeless
glass eyes stare down at us without reproach.

6

We who invented the clock and the metronome
cannot keep the calendar alive. We exist,
not on the edge of life but at its limits,
asking no pardon of the grass or the empty
shells which arrive and depart on each tide.

7

In the book of our history it will be recorded
that we murdered the earth. With the name
of a different crime tattooed on each finger
we walk out into the orchard and find
tiny mirrors hanging from the trees. Listen.
The leaves are screaming for help as they fall.

IV

The Choices

1

the whore has her knowledge
of man beyond rescue

to be held by many men in one night
knowing that not one of them
will hold anyone else that night

whether it is better to spend a life
not knowing what you want
or to spend a life knowing
exactly what you want
and that you will never have it

one of my hands was born in this kingdom
and one in the other

2

beauty cannot be looked at steadily
for very long
yet it is impossible to change one's voice
without changing one's life

how many times have I tried unsuccessfully
to forget what it was like to be a child

and do not condemn the liar for his lie
perhaps he was created to tell that lie
and we were created to listen

believe or not believe
as it was appointed

3

the forms of love are myriad as stars
and some men fall through space
for a lifetime
without touching any of them

love letters written in lemon juice
menus written in blood
the world is ruined no doubt
but even its bones are beautiful

and we are the guests of the slaughter
with words smeared on our lips like grease
our host is a knife hanging by a thread
turning as a beacon turns

when we have used up all the words
we will find the silences waiting for us
and choose one from among them

4

when I am in a room it is not empty
I am old enough to sing
cry dance or laugh without company
I can even sleep alone

the essential thing
is not that I have chosen to be a prisoner
but that I have chosen
what to be a prisoner of

and it was so simple
now that it is accomplished I forget
I ever made the choice

to live in the desert
this place which permits me to remain
where I have learned to call spiders
by their first names
little brothers of my darkness

where silence is nourishment
and each ghost carries
the ghost of tomorrow in his arms

where dawn arrives
like fire mixed with dry water
and every morning I am here to meet it
waiting to follow its instructions

did you know
when you took a train to a deserted station
you would find a woman with a child
did you know it would be yours
that you would carry it
the rest of your life

did you know you would find a talus slope
with a house a fence and a tree
all leaning in the same direction
that you would live there
watching a dead river reborn each year
and broken mountains crawling slowly to the sea

these are the upper lowlands
the lower slopes this is your home
the midden of your life

you could get here from anywhere
but once you are here
there are many places you can never go

if you leave you will leave all you have
all you can account for
some artifacts of triumph
scattered among the precious shards
of your disasters

SAN JUAN'S DAY

during summer in these latitudes
one disappointment is as good as another

each year when the rains come
we are convinced by the sophistries of water
that the dust will not be back

and each year it returns unerringly
falling upon us
like the patience we have forgotten we possess

1

the wind keeps trying to do things to me
but I resist it
with the seriousness of my body

in one minute I have resisted
a thousand suggestions
the desire for warm lubricity
somewhere to bury myself
and in dying
know the parietal image of thunder
which shakes my thighs in spasms
and speaks only to me

2

courage is a quality I do not
possess very much of
but I admire it God knows I admire it

I have seen it from a distance
and from the corner of my eye
when one man rises
while others are in shelter
Hypnos waking
we are now approaching
the instant when death is most violent
and life is most clearly defined

eyes dilated in such a dream
what do they see

3

the best most men can hope for
is a sheet turning its hands down at night
a moist mouth in the darkness
and at the end of a public life
a private death

but you and I have created a quiet place
where the fire talks to itself
disturbing no one
and shadows grow on the wall

a quiet place
with your voice in it and a child

the vine of my manhood
trained on your trellis and blooming

4

I have been selfish always
what I do I do for myself alone
a minor kind of courage

yet my hands have learned
to fit your face
like the frame for a picture of snowy hills
hands which can be crippled
perishable hands

and we live together
surrounded by the luxury of shipwreck
a pride in scars

when I can no longer stand I will fall
when the words are gone
I will take silence as my province

until then we resist and remain
while sand runs down
in little rivers to the sea

at a distance the city whines all night
but here in a quiet place
under a tin roof waiting for rain
we wrap ourselves in our love and go to sleep

MERMAID

I send my pride out to you
on the end of a string
but it is not bait enough

I send my love
and you turn away

I send words again and again
but they come back empty

later
when my pain
creeps over the surface of the water
you leap to me
saying *lover lover*
enter my crippled room

her hair burns and is never consumed
her eyebrows are infinite
her eyelids are blue clouds
over blue mountains at dawn
her eyes know separate worlds
yet both speak the same language

her nostrils divide a kingdom between them
her lips are beaches on whose sand I sleep
her teeth are tiny fingers
her tongue is silence
at the mention of her silence I listen

her ears are mornings which hold
the secrets of afternoons in their arms
her temples are pools of water in the mirage
her chin is a pear I take in my mouth
her neck holds bruises as if they were born there
her breasts are twins
one remembers what the other forgets

her arms are light reflected on water
her hands are braided milk
her fingers are keys to the locks of my body
her fingernails are moons rising in wax
her thighs are a nest of dark pearls
seeing in all directions

her legs rise up early to surround me
her knees are stirrups for my shoulders
her ankles know the truth and repeat it
her feet walk on air as if it were water
her odor is the odor of the young syringa

inside her is a secret place
where a star about to explode is waiting

when the crows fly away
with their compassion
and I remain to eat
whatever is left of my heart

I think of my love
with the odor of salt
of my love who holds me in her eyes
as if I were whole and beautiful

and I think of those
who walk the streets all night
frantic with desire and bruised
by the terrible small lips of rain

I touch you
as a blind man touches the dice
and finds he has won

FOR LOIS

love
it takes so long
to learn who we are
then it is always the wrong one

I am growing old
and no one comes to my rescue

the weak are spectators
the powerful are somewhere else
managing their own desires

I am so tired
dull scissors could finish my story

love
if I could only
be sure about the future
I would sleep a little while
or be dead a little while
and wake to find you

once a year
when infallible toads
begin to sing
all the spiders who left me
return and I make room for them

I am too proud
to mention their long absence

then the owls
send a message in code
from saguaro to saguaro
and the toads stop singing

a sea of warm air
rolls over quickly and relaxes
we wait for the promised rain
for the second coming
of water

each time it arrives
like the flood and I know
I have not wasted my life

spiders still come
to my house for shelter

1

a small child of a wind
stumbles toward me down the arroyo
lost and carrying no light
tearing its sleeves
on thorns of the palo verde
talking to itself
and to the dark shapes it touches
searching for what it has not lost
and will never find
searching
and lonelier
than even I can imagine

the moon sleeps
with her head on the buttocks of a young hill
and you lie before me
under moonlight as if under water
oh my desert
the coolness of your face

2

men are coming inland to you
soon they will make you the last resort
for tourists who have
nowhere else to go

what will become of the coyote
with eyes of topaz
moving silently to his undoing
the ocotillo
flagellant of the wind
the deer climbing with dignity
further into the mountains
the huge and delicate saguaro

what will become of those who cannot learn
the terrible knowledge of cities

3

years ago I came to you as a stranger
and have never been worthy
to be called your lover or to speak your name
loveliest
most silent sanctuary
more fragile than forests
more beautiful than water

I am older and uglier
and full of the knowledge
that I do not belong to beauty
and beauty does not belong to me
I have learned to accept
whatever men choose to give me
or whatever they choose to withhold
but oh my desert
yours is the only death I cannot bear

V

The Fourteenth Anniversary

> And Jacob served seven years for Rachel;
> and they seemed unto him but a few days,
> for the love he had to her.
> *Genesis 29:20*

1

in winter when each day is harvested
we come out of darkness into the light
of a fire built from what is left over

with our decisions postponed
and our shadows no longer wearing
their daytime shoes

it is as if we have something to say
to the fire but we keep forgetting

later when you are asleep
I walk through these rooms
adjusting my mask to the silence

the fire is dying and outside
the moon is a knock waiting with no door

2

we came out of childhood into a room
with all its vases waiting for flowers
into a luxury of absent flowers
and the light was different

how easily the moon insinuates herself
among the clouds how shyly she undresses
and how quickly she reclines

with my hands reaching
to lock the door which was opening
in the moment it was opening I noticed
the simplicities
I had removed from my pockets
and left on a table by the wrong bed
for anyone to see

these things have never been resolved
will never be resolved

3

do not believe what they say about me
it is true but it is not the truth

the truth is hidden
in the brain of a green bird who cannot sing
the truth is in one seed of a pomegranate
among thousands of pomegranates

the truth is on the moon's white lips
as she sinks into the sea
strange silent lady
worshipped by men who lie in the mud
beneath her slender foot

4

finding they cannot walk on water
some men sink while others
go into the desert and never return

the sea is willing the sea accepts everything
but those who walk in the desert
travel in circles and arrive
always at the same place
with dawn close behind them
trailing frail light as if it were hair

walking in the desert
I have begun to see into my body's rivers
whose banks are ivory and pearl
with bridges of muscle stretching above them
pulsing in time to the music of the nerves

inside the bones the light
is failing but I see small things
crawling over the floor on urgent business
like beetles on strings

I see into my sex and it is not
a jewel it is a small fire
tended by old men who are dying

a small fire in a great dark house
where the wind comes through the walls
and a book turns its own pages carefully
so as not to miss anything

I read in the book that all the glory
of the kings I have not known
and all the beauty of the queens
will die when that fire dies

5

then I take my tongue to your body
letting it wander blind over your ribs
as if each were one string of a harp
leaving no string untouched

we reach our hands deep into one another
and if they come up at all
they come up full of poetry the moon
a few stars and a silence rinsed in blood

who dares speak against that silence
let him speak

I have loved you honestly
with all my crooked heart and gently
as darkness comes to water
and in passion with the storm

of all the nothings I have ever said
one word remains
I wear it as a wafer on my tongue
it is your name

6

bind up the sagging breasts of morning
oh my darling let the light in

your hair is more beautiful than dawn

we have arrived years later
at the starting place
now we shall begin again

*This book of poems was set in the Linotype
cutting of Palatino, a typeface designed by Hermann Zapf
and named for the sixteenth-century Italian scribe.
It is printed on Olde Style wove antique paper directly
from the type by Heritage Printers, Inc.
The book was designed by Gary Gore.*

Pitt Poetry Series